TEST COLOR PAGE

NUMBERS

9 6 2 5 7 8 1 4 3 0

Zero

One

1

Two

2

Three

3

Four

4

Five

5

Six

6

Seven

7

Eight

8

Nine
9

Ten

10

LETTERS & PROFESSIONS

Z

B

C

n

A

T

Actor

Aa

Baker

Bb

Construction worker

Cc

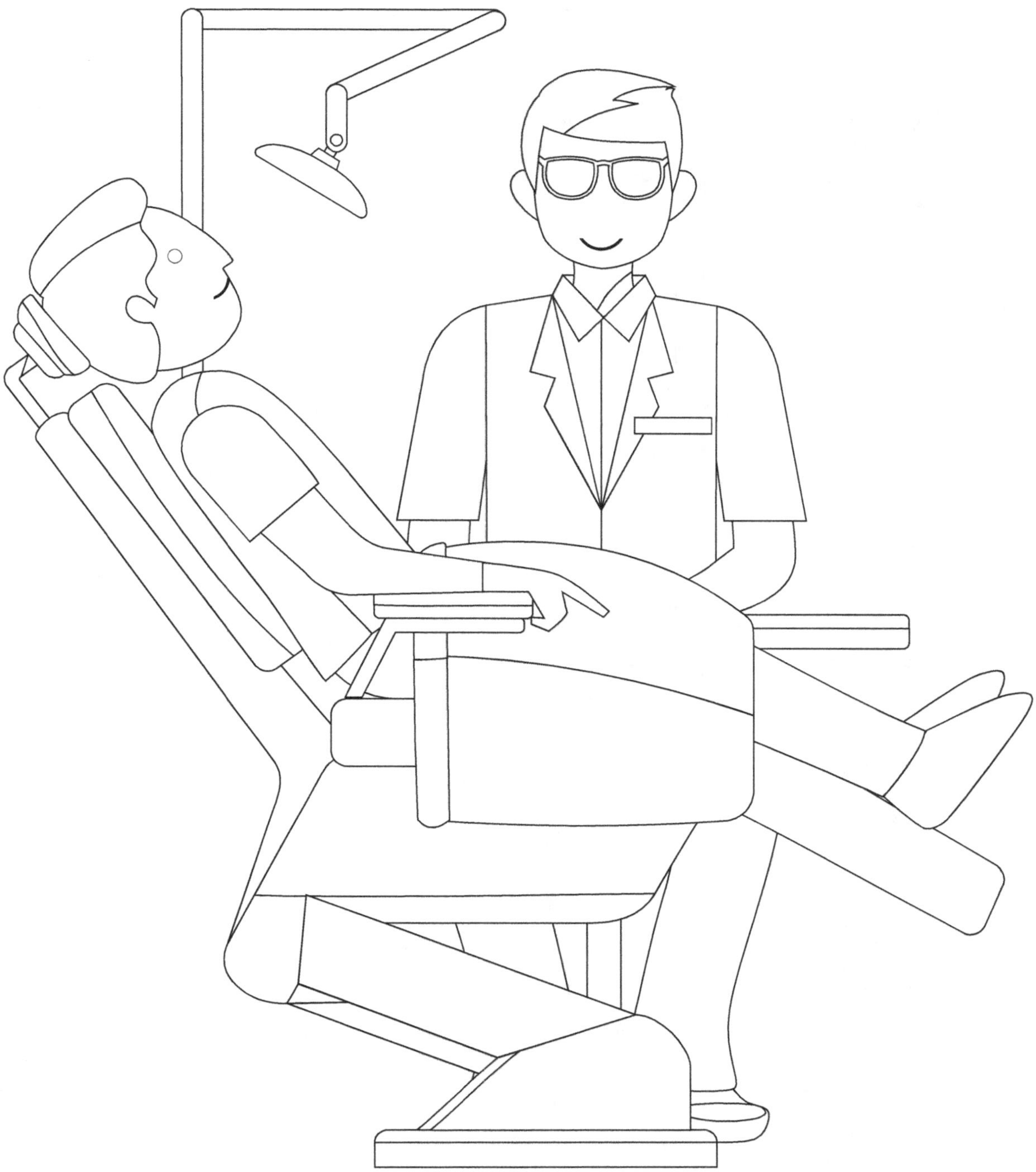

Dentist

D d

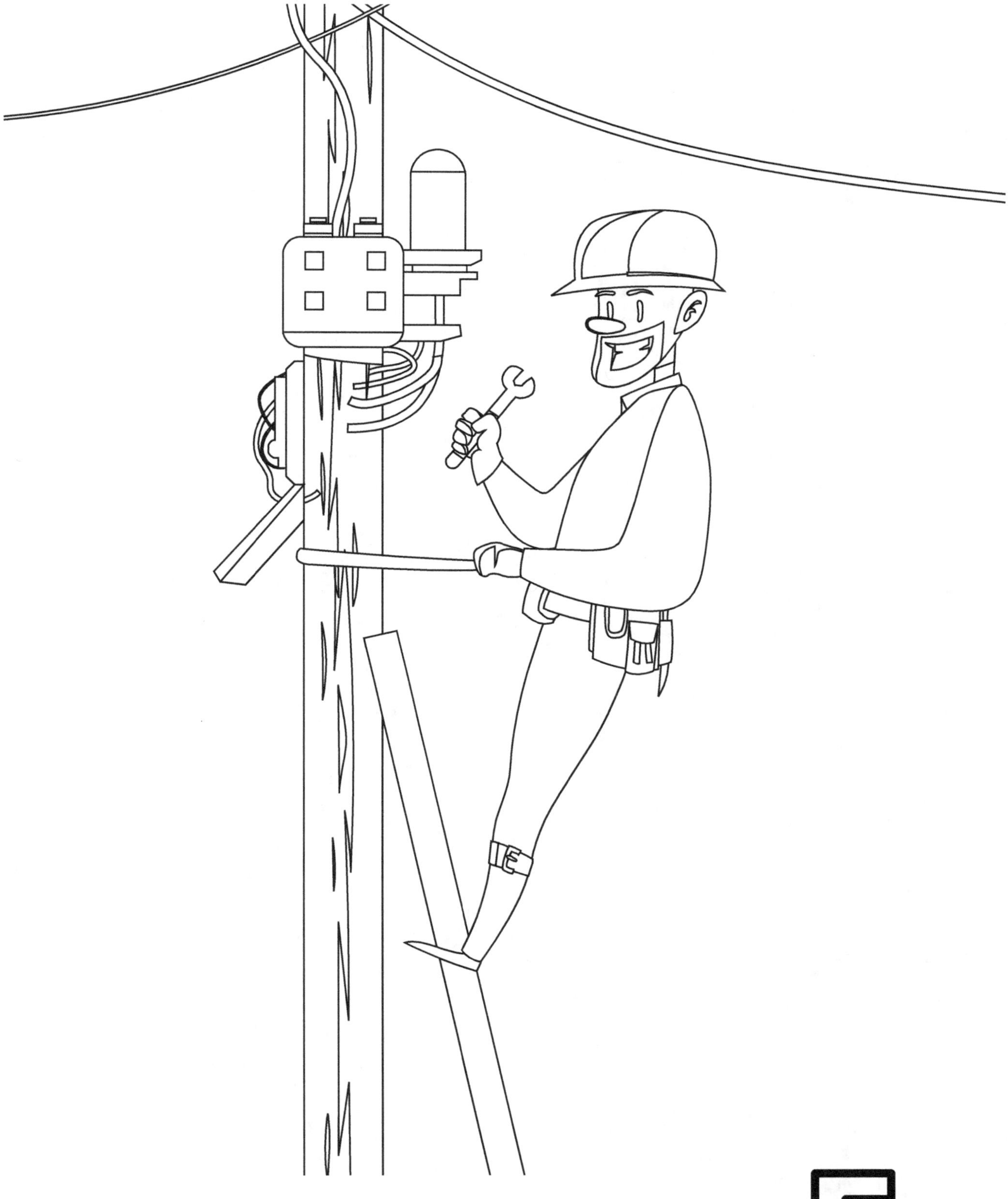

Electrician

Ee

Farmer

Ff

Guitarist

Gg

Hairdresser

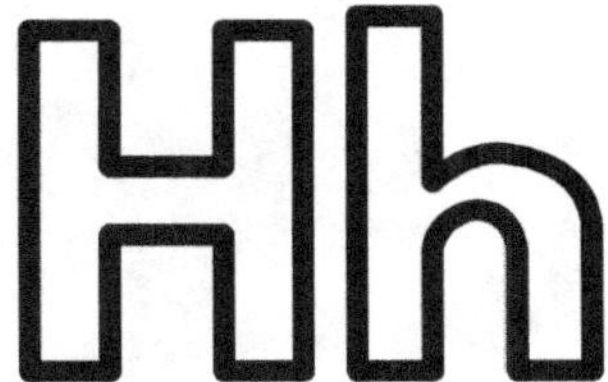

Interior designer

Journalist

Jj

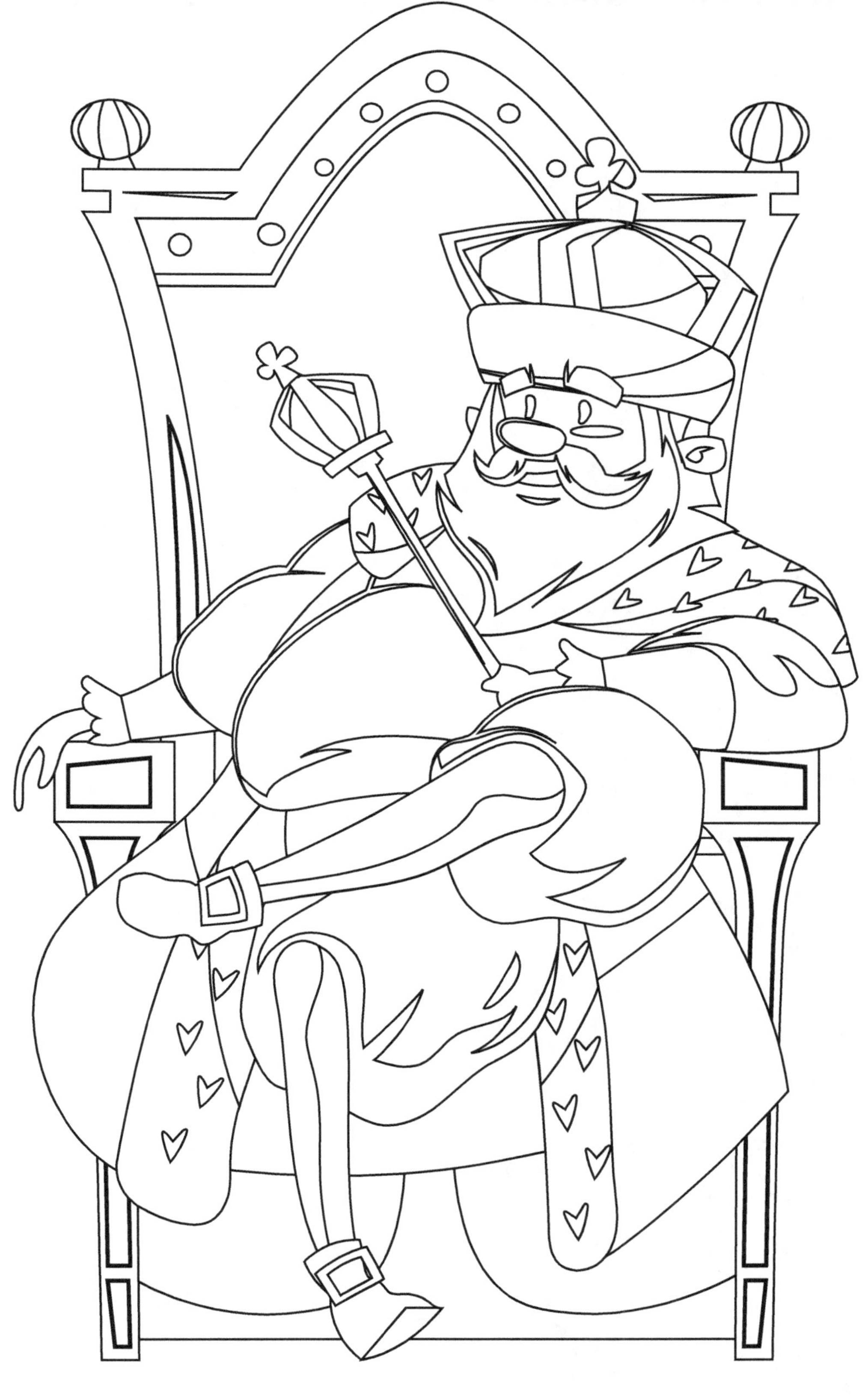

King

Kk

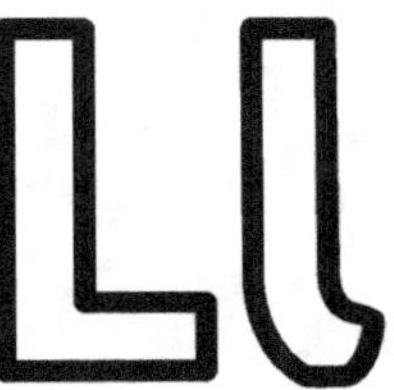

Lecturer

Ll

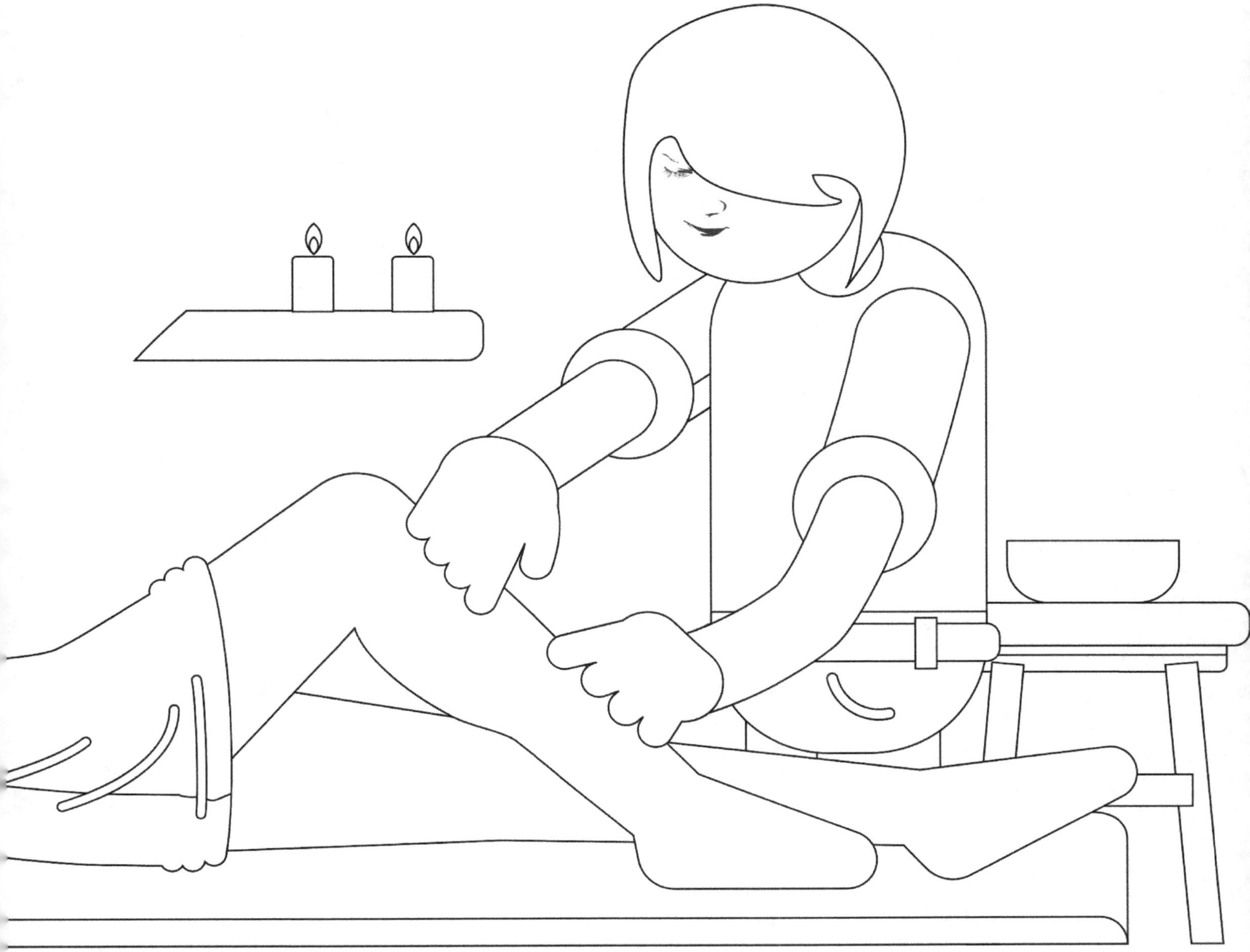

Masseur

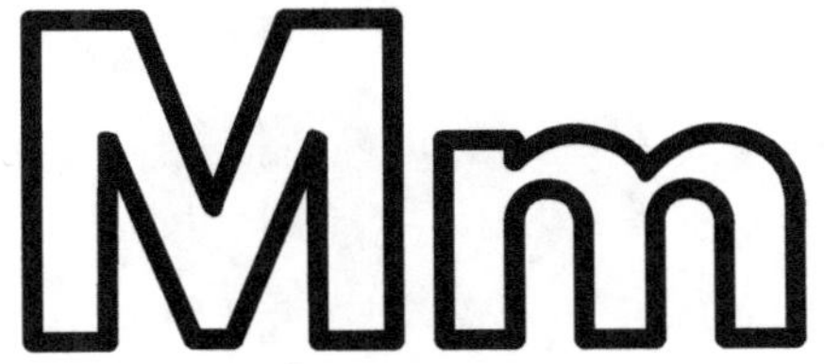

Mm

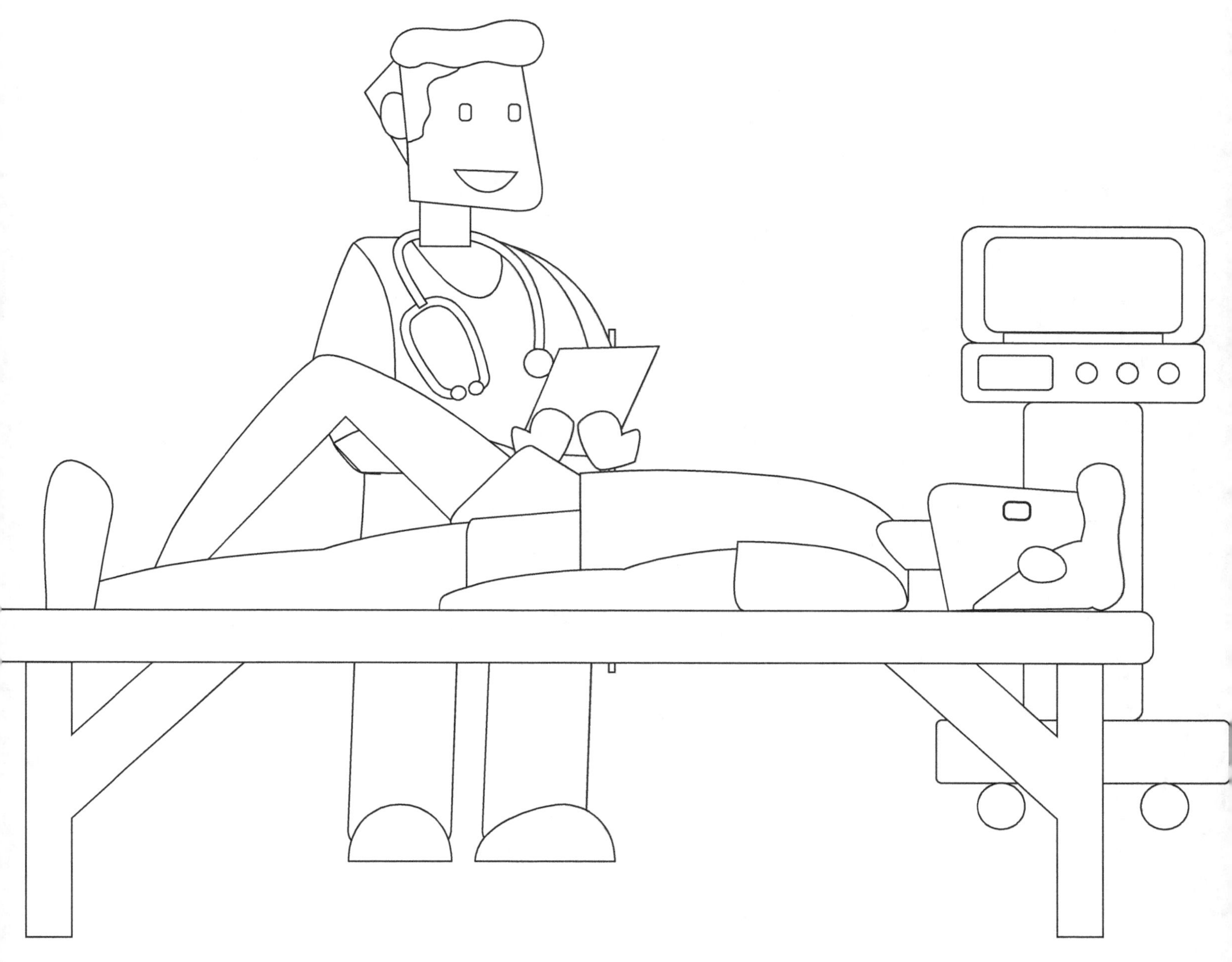

Nurse

Nn

4 M C
8 2 O
2 5 O
3 4 C
0 7 C
Optician
Oo

Policeman

Pp

Queen

Qq

Repairer

Rr

Scientist

Ss

Trainer

Tt

Usher

Vet

V v

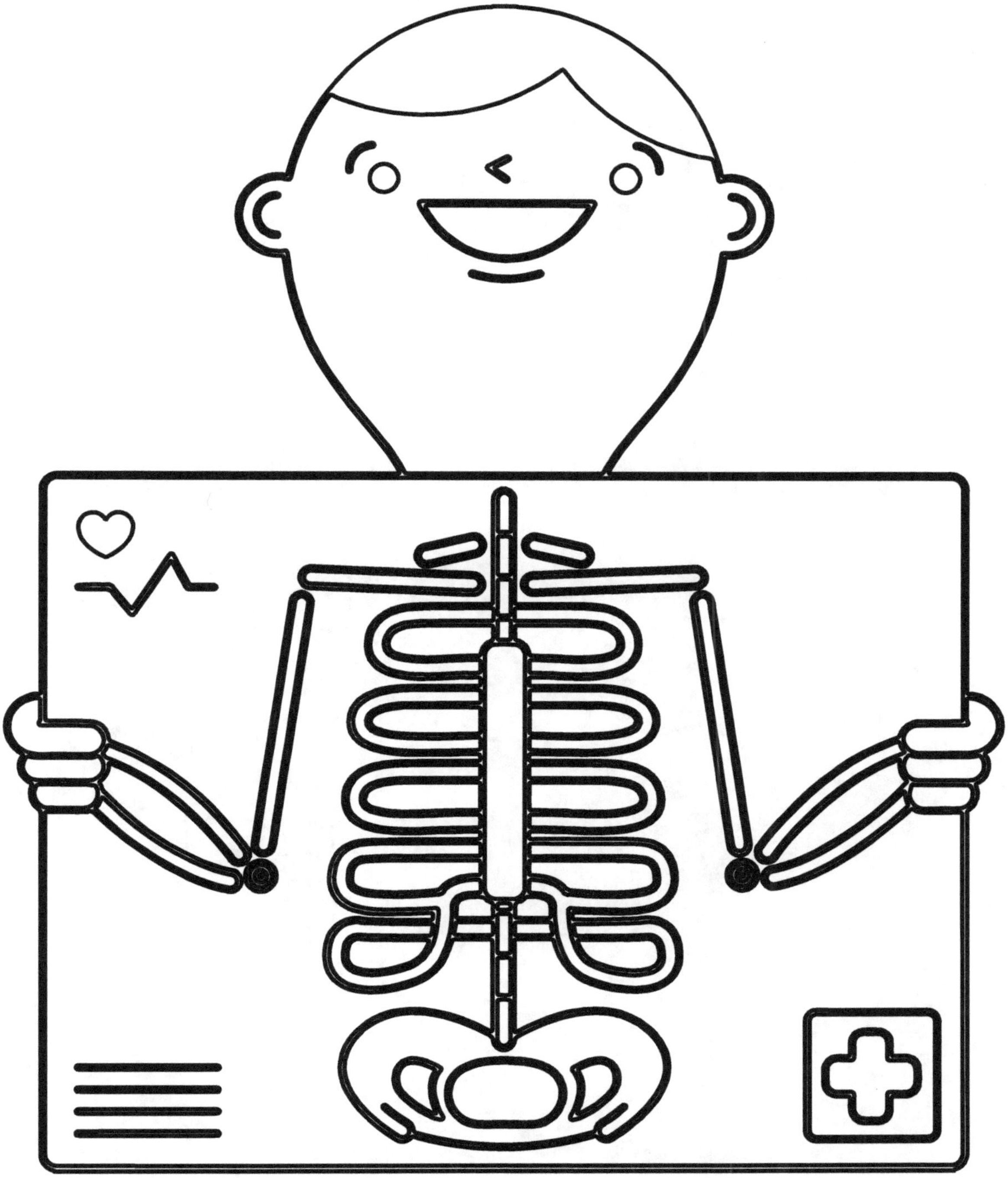

X-ray
technician

Xx

Yardman

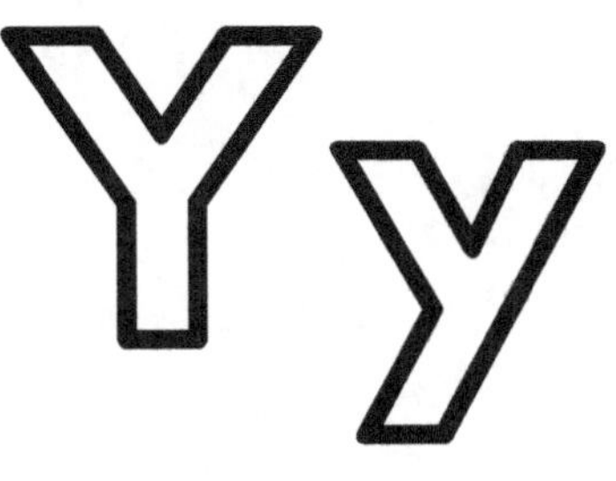

Yy

Waitner

Ww

Zoologist

Zz